The Pet Psychic™

CANINE SPIRIT GUIDES
ORACLE CARDS

BY
RON ASH

The Dachshund
PLAYFULLNESS

CLAIRALIENCE
SPIRITUAL GUIDANCE THROUGH SMELL
MONEY THROUGH PARTNERSHIP
Three of Clubs

The Bull Terrier
SILLINESS

ATTACHMENTS
FRIENDLY AND FUN LOVING
THINGS MAY NOT BE AS THEY SEEM
Jack of Diamonds

The Flat-Coated Retriever
DETERMINATION

ENTHUSIASM
OPTIMISTIC AND GOOD HUMORED
LOOK BEFORE YOU LEAP
Eight of Spades

The Dalmatian
PERFORMANCE

ENDURANCE
ALERTNESS AND INTELLIGENCE
FINANCIAL ALLIANCE
Ten of Spades

The Chow Chow
COMPANIONSHIP

POWERFUL
AFFECTIONATE AND DEVOTED
DREAMS ARE MANIFESTING
Nine of Hearts

The Boston Terrier
TEMPERANCE

LIVELENESS
CALMNESS AND BALANCE
MIND YOUR TONGUE
Three of Hearts

The German Shepherd Dog
LOYALTY

MANDATES
DIRECT AND FEARLESS
TRUST YOUR INSTINCTS
Four of Clubs

The Irish Setter
STABILITY

TRANSFERANCE
LIGHTHEARTED AND ENERGETIC
HEALTH, WEALTH AND HAPPINESS
Ace of Clubs

The Basset Hound
VERSATILITY

CONCILIATORY
CONFORMITY AND OBEDIENCE
WATCH YOUR HEALTH AND FINANCES
Four of Spades

The Shiba Inu
AGILITY

INDEPENDENCE
KEEN SENSES
FLEXIBILITY ATTRACTS A NEW LOVE
Nine of Clubs

The Polish Lowland Sheepdog
SPIRITEDNESS

PROTECTION
SUSPICIOUS OF STRANGERS
INSIST ON MATURITY AND RELIABILITY
Jack of Spades

The Basenji
ELEGANCE

FASTIDIOUS
ALOOF AND FROLICSOME
FINANCIAL HELP AND BUSINESS SUCCESS
Six of Clubs

The Papillon
DAINTINESS

OUTGOING
JOVIAL AND ATTENTIVE
INHERITANCE OR FINACIAL INCREASE
Four of Diamonds

The Japanese Chin
FOCUS

FAVORITISM
CENTER OF ATTENTION
CONSIDER RELATIONSHIP COUNSELING
Six of Diamonds

The Parson Russell Terrier
READINESS

TENACIOUS
CONFIDENCE AND ENDURANCE
A RELIABLE FRIEND IS APPRECIATED
Jack of Hearts

The Bernese Mountain Dog
RESILIENCE

TOLERANCE
DROVING AND DRAFTING
THINGS ARE COMING TO A HEAD
Ace of Spades

The English Cocker Spaniel
EXPRESSIVENESS

CHARACTER
INVESTIGATIVE AND MOBILE
EMPHASIS ON FORTUNE AND TRAVEL
Ten of Diamonds

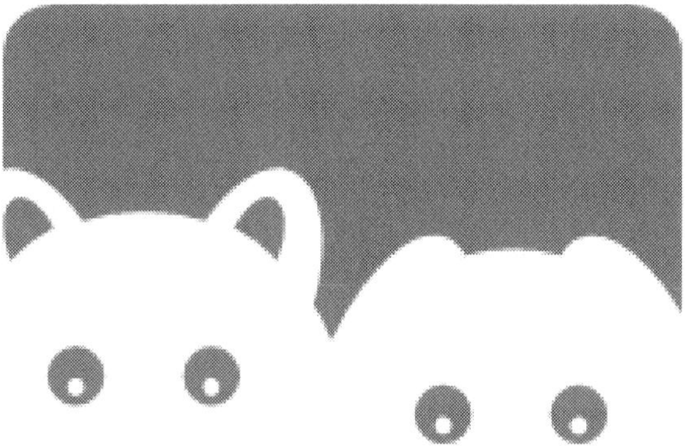

The Saluki
ADHERANCE

STEALTHY
PATIENCE AND CONSISTENCY
A NEWCOMER WITH MATERNAL INSTICTS
Queen of Hearts

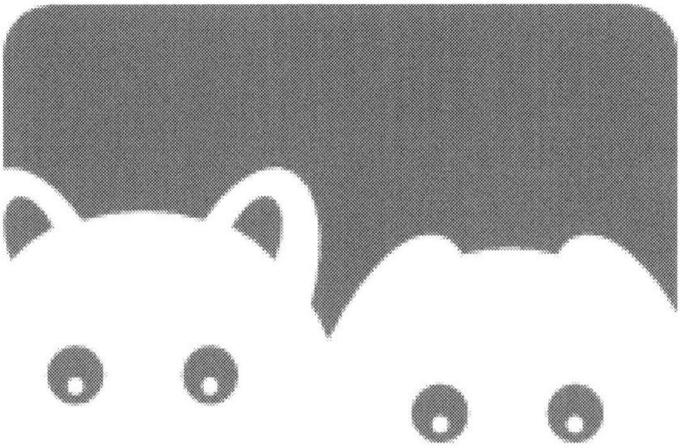

The Labrador Retriever
ADAPTABILITY

GRATIFIER
GUIDANCE AND ENLIGHTENMENT
A RELATIONSHIP REJECTED BY FRIENDS
Two of Diamonds

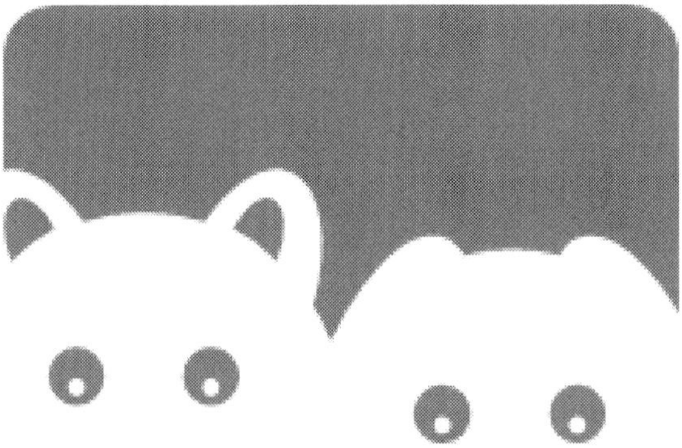

The Chinese Crested
DESIRE

SENSATIVITY
OBSERVENT AND TENDER
GRADUAL PROGRESS AND IMPROVEMENT
Six of Spades

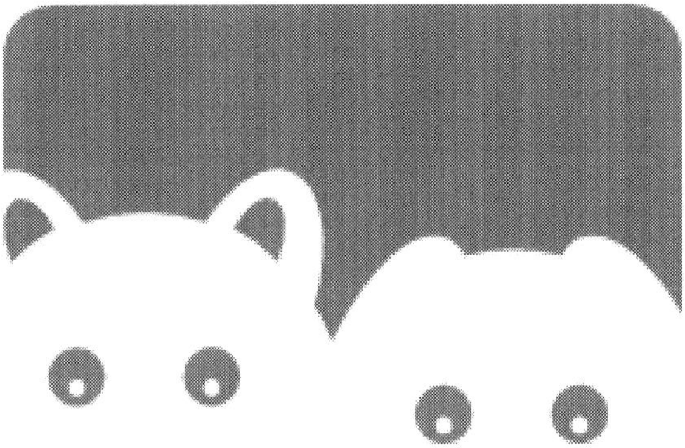

The Lakeland Terrier
INSTICTIVENESS

CRAMMER
WISDOM AND FOLLY
LUCK AND UNEXPECTED MONEY
Ten of Clubs

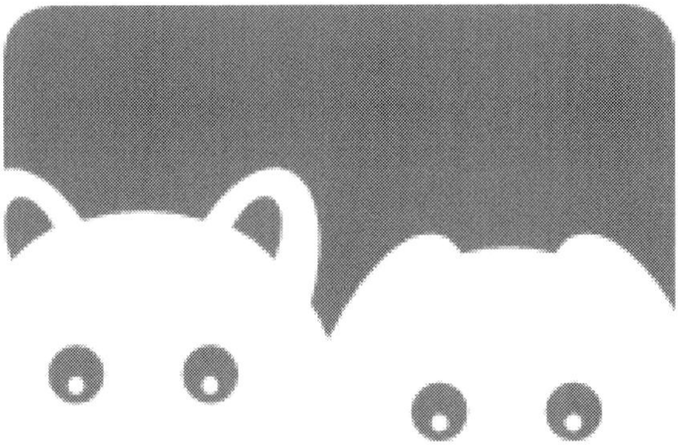

The Siberian Husky
PREDATORY

COOPERATION
AGREEABLE AND OUTGOING
GOOD LUCK AND HAPPINESS
Ten of Hearts

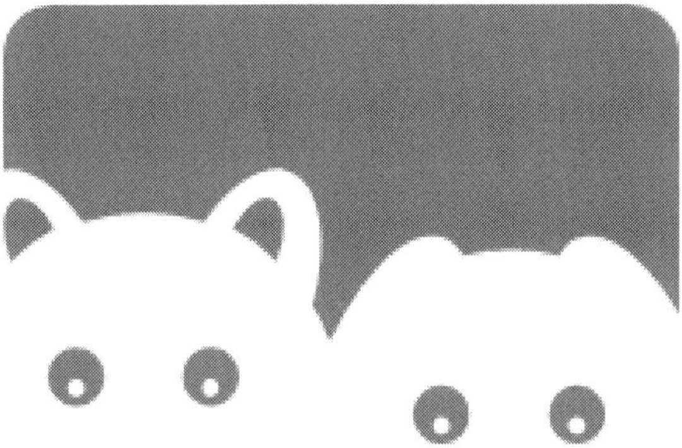

The Newfoundland
VALOR

HEROISM
GROUNDED AND FLUID
SUCCESS IN BUSINESS AND FAMILY
Five of Diamonds

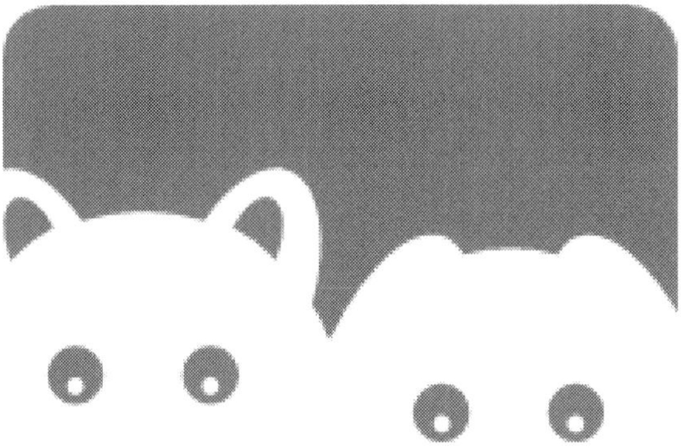

The Yorkshire Terrier
INVESTIGATIVE

SOCIALIZATION
ENERGETIC AND RESOLUTE
FEW SETBACKS AND EVENTUAL SUCCESS
Five of Spades

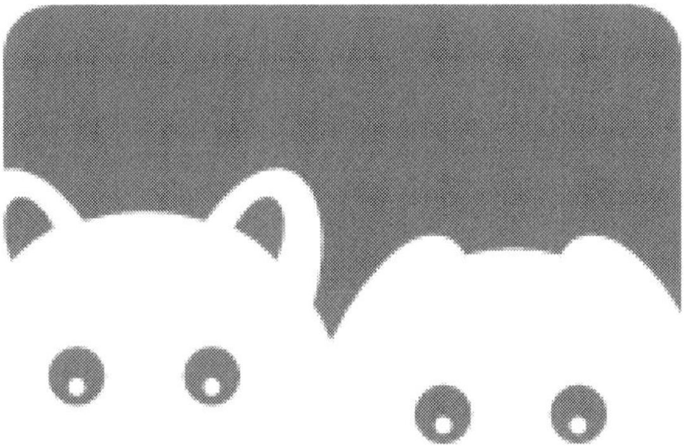

The Welsh Corgi
STURDINESS

CONFORMITY
COMPETITION AND TRADITION
VISITING WITH FAMILY AND FRIENDS
Eight of Hearts

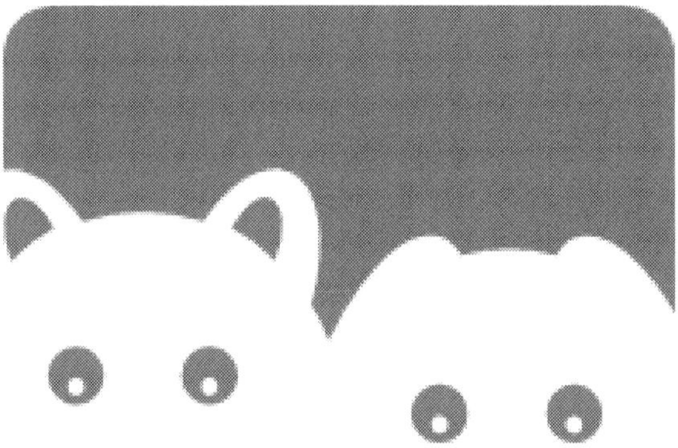

The Old English Sheepdog
LABORIOUS

ATHELETIC
INTENSIVE AND STRENUOUS WORK
TAKE TIME TO MAKE BETTER CHOICES
Five of Hearts

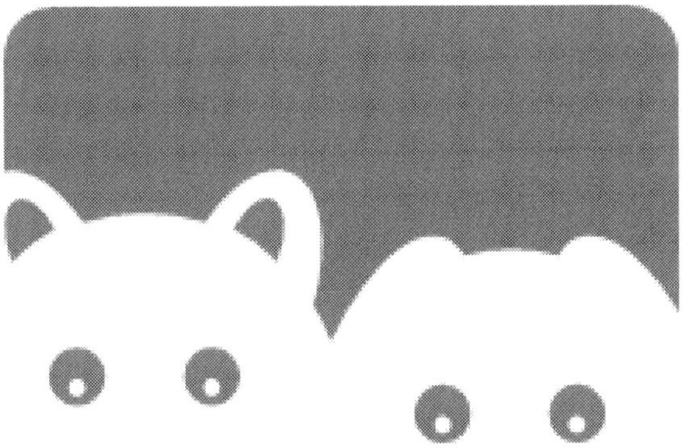

The Border Collie
INTUITION

TELEKINETIC
MOVING BY MOTION OR BY GAZE
GREAT ADVICE IS COMING SOON
King of Hearts

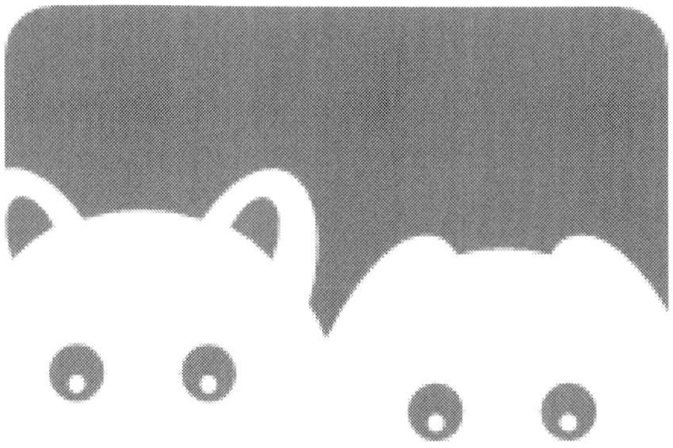

The Boxer
CONDITIONING

MESSENGER
PATIENT AND SPIRITED
STAY IN GRATITUDE AND APPRECIATION
Seven of Spades

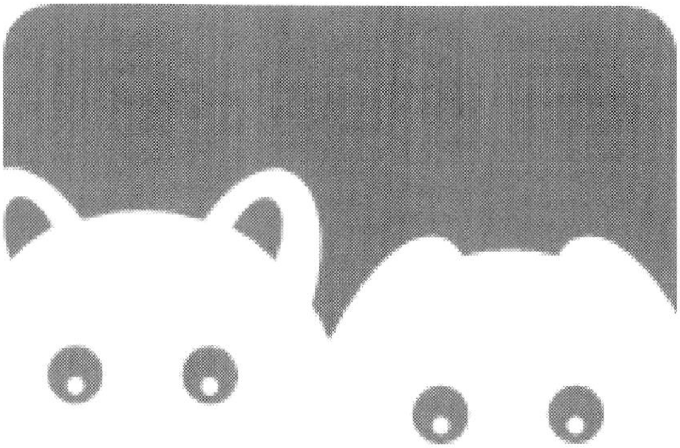

The Australian Shepherd
PURPOSEFUL

ANIMATED
ADAPTABILITY AND AGILITY
PLEASANT SUPRISES OR NEW GIFTS
Seven of Diamonds

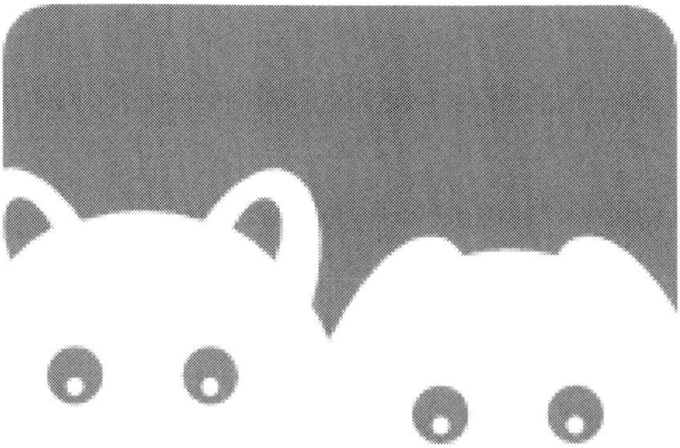

The Dandie Dinmount Terrier
SOULFULNESS

CONFIDENCE
AN INFLATED EGO AND SELF-ASSURANCE
CAREFULLY EVALUATE PARTNERSHIPS
Three of Spades

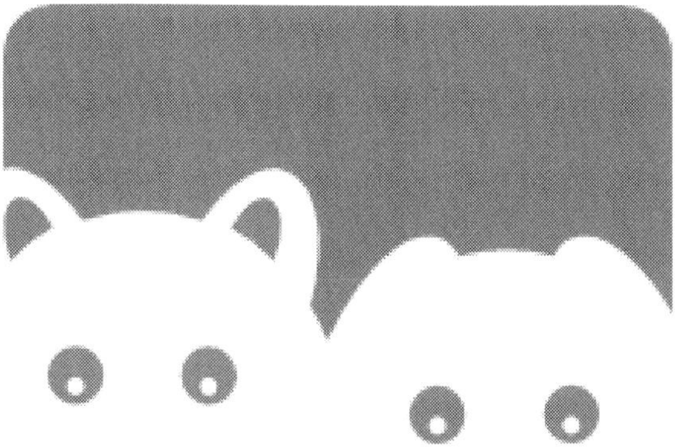

The Rottweiler
FORCEFULNESS

TASKMASTER
RESPONSIBILITY AND DISCIPLINE
REMAIN FAITHFUL AND KEEP PROMISES
Seven of Hearts

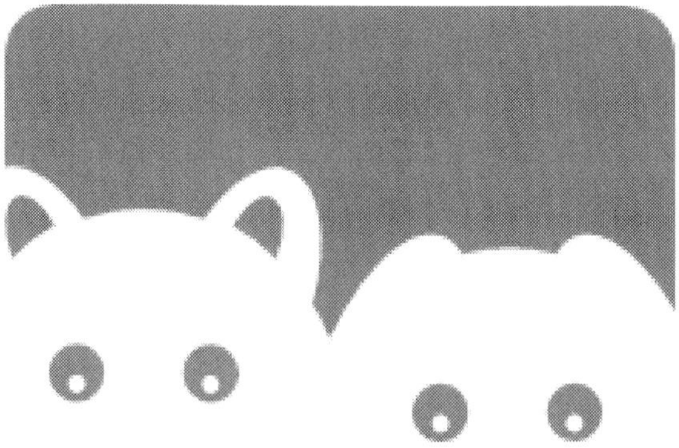

The Miniature Schnauzer

DISTINGUISHED

OVERSEER
SMART AND CONSISTENTLY CHEERFUL
MAJOR CHANGES ARE ON THERE WAY
Four of Hearts

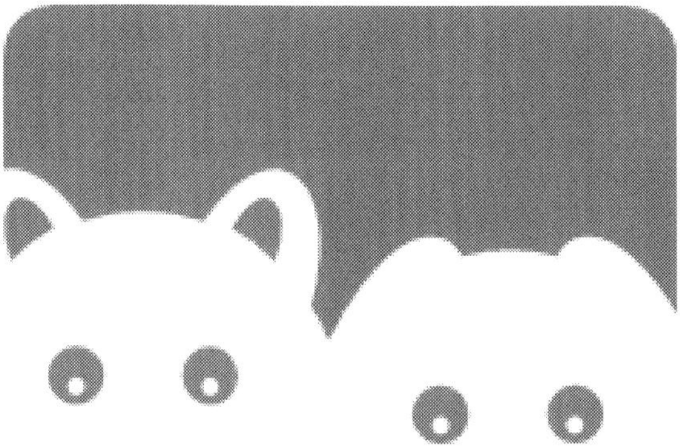

The Golden Retriever
ASSISTANCE

WORKABILITY
A GUIDING LIGHT AND SAVIOR
INFORMATION OR MONEY IS ON THE WAY
Ace of Diamonds

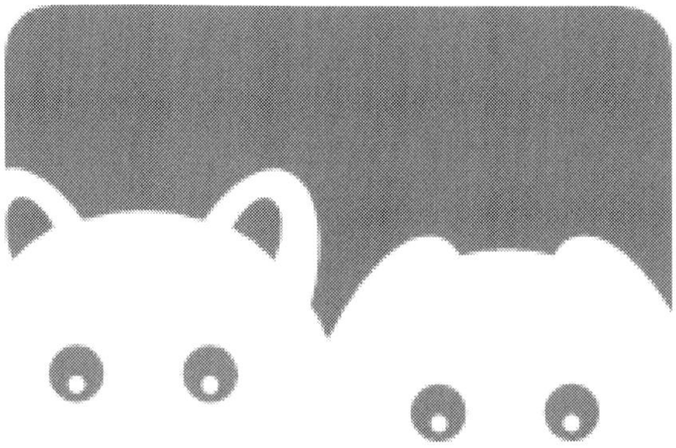

The American Cocker Spaniel
JOYOUS

BALANCED
SPEED AND ENDURANCE
UNEXPECTED HELP HAS ARRIVED
Six of Hearts

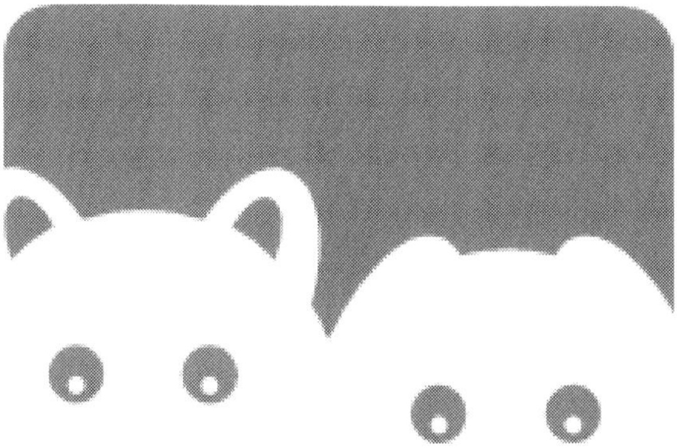

The Chihuahua
GRACEFUL

SWIFT
GENTLE AND SERENE
DIFFICULT BUT NEEDED CHANGES
Two of Spades

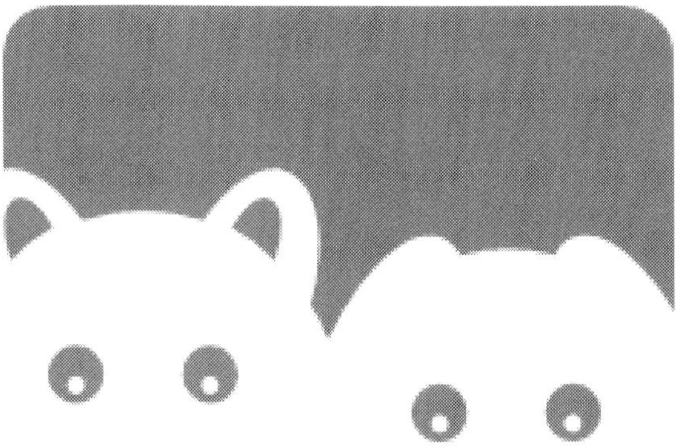

The Bouvier Des Flanders
STEADINESS

UNWAVERING
A FEARLESS GUARDIAN
MODERATION IS THE KEY
Queen of Diamonds

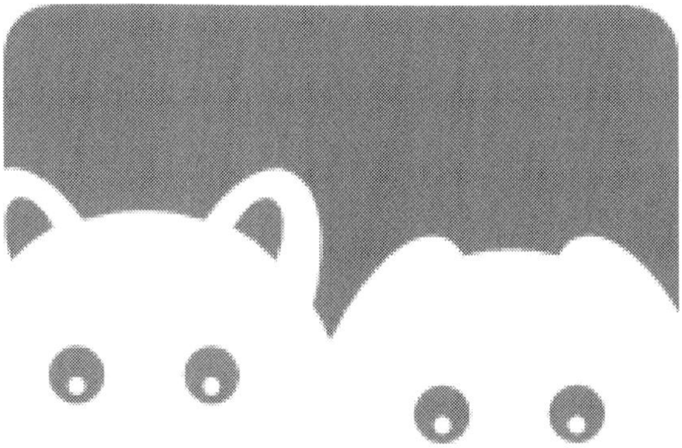

The Pomeranian
EXTROVERTED

SMUG
**REQUIRES A GREAT DEAL OF ATTENTION
HEATED DISSCUSIONS AND DEBATE**
Three of Diamonds

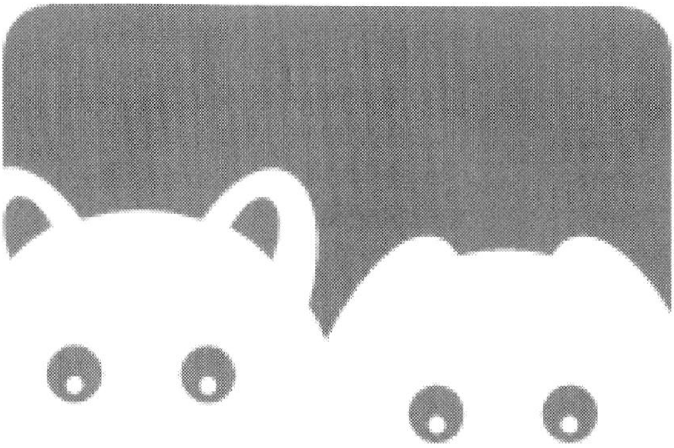

The St. Bernard
DIGNIFIED

STEADFAST
DRAWN TO HELP THE LOST AND HELPLESS
PROSPERITY AND SUCCCESS
Seven of Clubs

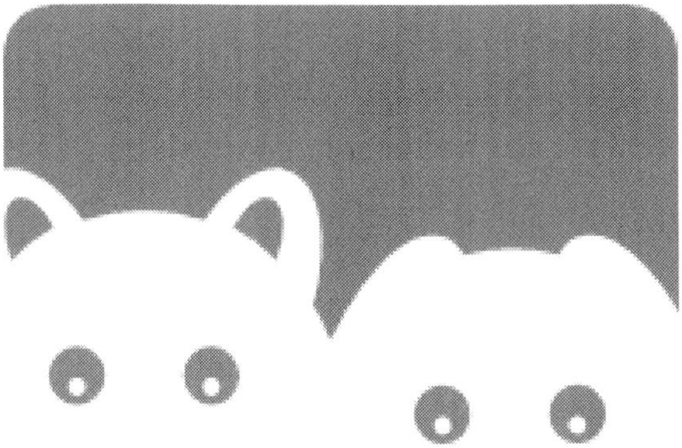

The Afgan Hound
ARISTOCRATIC

CLAIRVOYANT
EXTREMELY INDIVIDUALIED CHARACTER
FINANCIAL UPS AND DOWNS
Eight of Diamonds

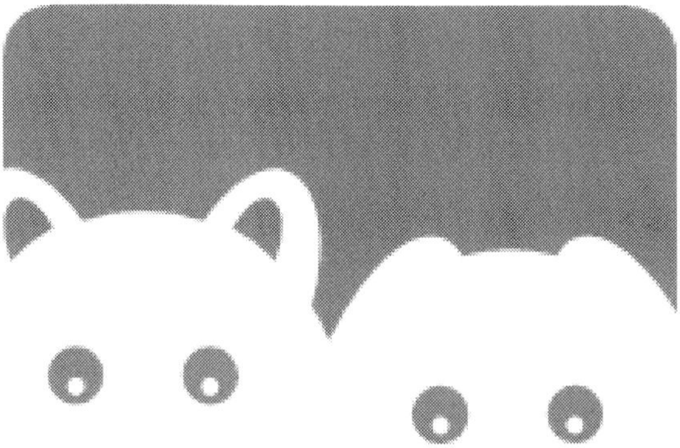

The Miniature Pinscher
EXCITEMENT

CURIOSITY
STUBBORN AND CLEVER
CONFIDENCE CREATES ATTRACTION
Queen of Clubs

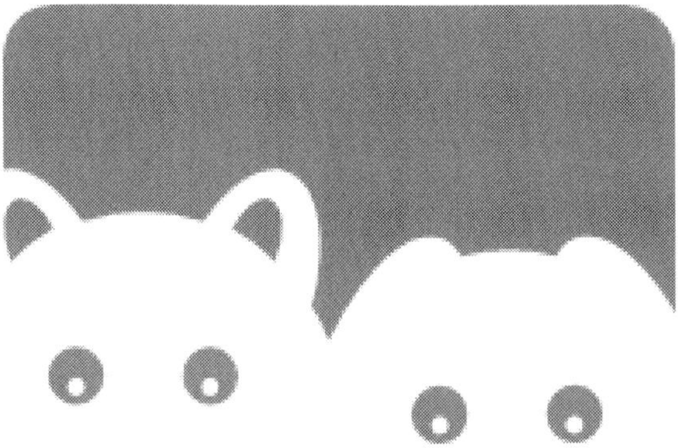

The Airedale Terrier
USEFULNESS

CHARMING
RESILENT AND DUTIFUL
BE RESISTENT TO JEALOUSY AND GREED
Eight of Clubs

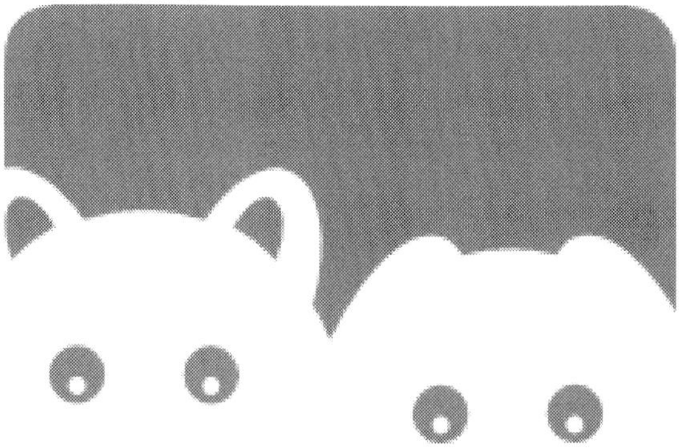

The Shetland Sheepdog
DEVOTION

PASSIVE
MULTIFACETED AND UNASSUMING
A GENEROUS AFFECTIONATE PARTNER
King of Clubs

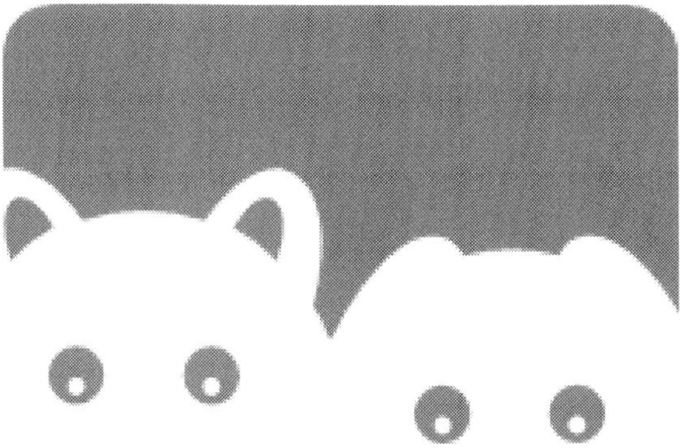

The Akita
THERAPIST

DARING
CALM TO BOUNCY AND AGGRESSIVE
THE START OF A NEW ROMANCE
Ace of Hearts

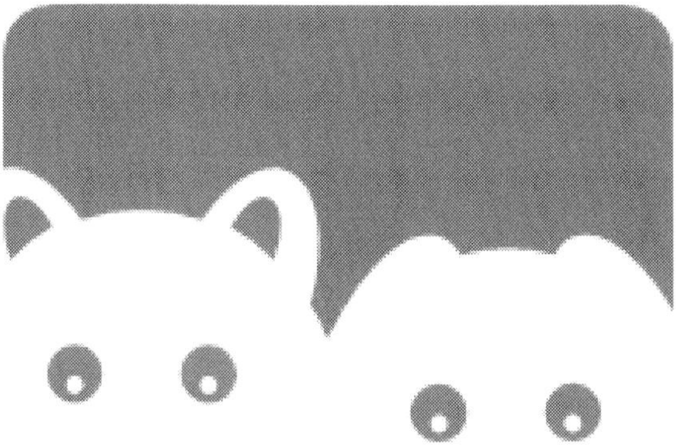

The Pug
ENTERTAINER

EVEN-TEMPERS
OUTGOING WITH A LOVING DISPOSITION
DISAPPOINTMENT AND OPPOSITION
Two of Clubs

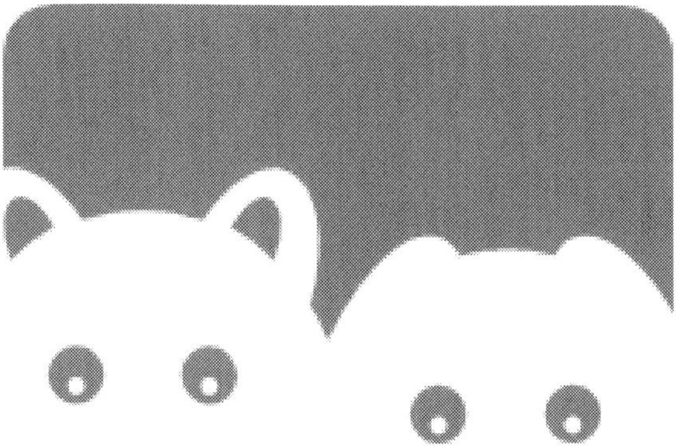

The French Bulldog
COMEDIAN

AFFECTIONATE
ACTIVE AND ALERT
A DEPENDABLE FRIEND EMERGES
Jack of Clubs

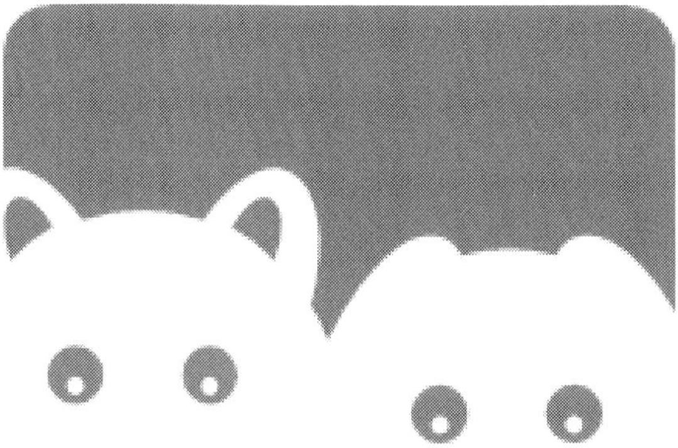

The Bulldog
EQUABLENESS

RESOLUTE
FORMING STRONG BONDS
STUBORN AND INFLUENTIAL LEADERSHIP
King of Diamonds

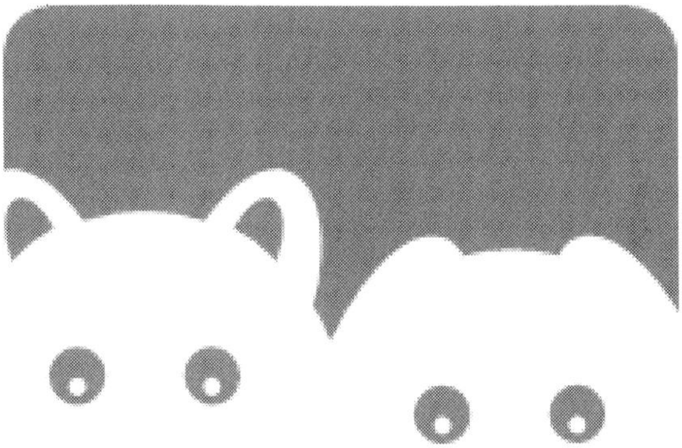

The Poodle
EXQUISITNESS

ASTUTENESS
**FINDING EQUITABLE RESOLUTION
NEW FRIENDS AND MARRITAL SUCCESS**
Five of Clubs

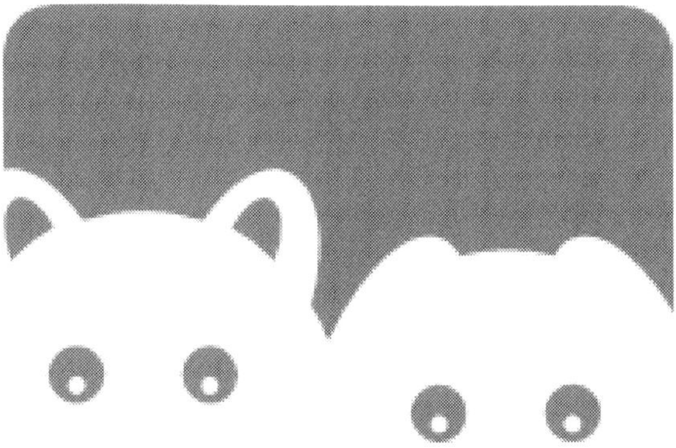

The Beagle
HAPPINESS

MISCHIEVIOUS
CURIOUS AND COMEDIC
NEW AMBITIOUS AUTHORATATIVE BOSS
King of Spades

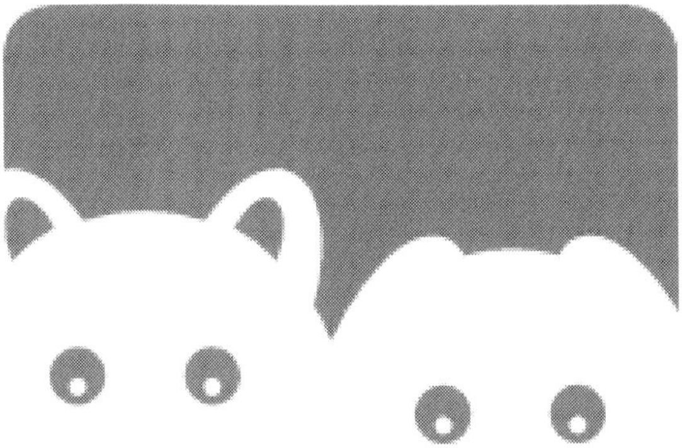

The Bichon Frise
CHEERFULNESS

INQUISATIVE
CLARITY AND UNDERSTANDING
BEWARE OF A DECEITFUL STRANGER
Queen of Spades

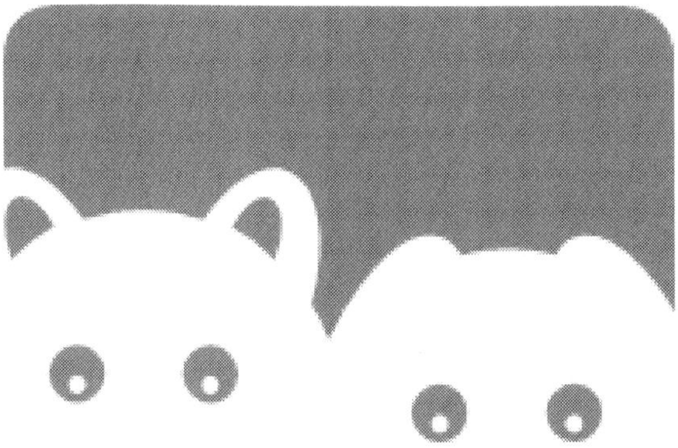

The Maltese
TENDERNESS

DYNAMIC
REFINEMENT AND REWARD
NEW BUSINESS OPPORTUNITIES
Nine of Diamonds

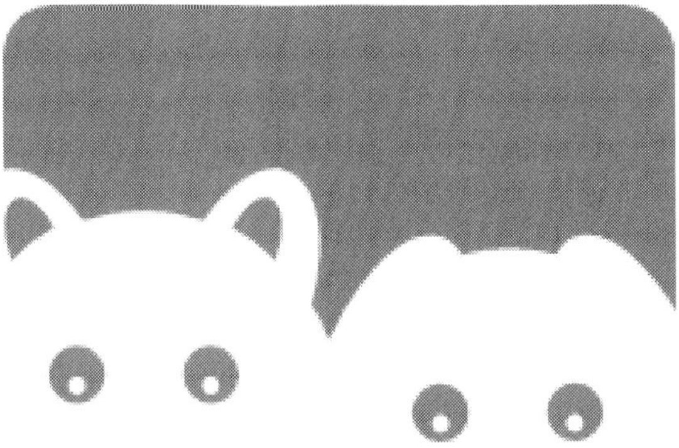

The Cavalier King Charles Spaniel
ELEGANCE

TRUSTWORTHY
FAMILY AND FRIENDS
THINK POSITIVE AND RAISE VIBRATION
Nine of Spades

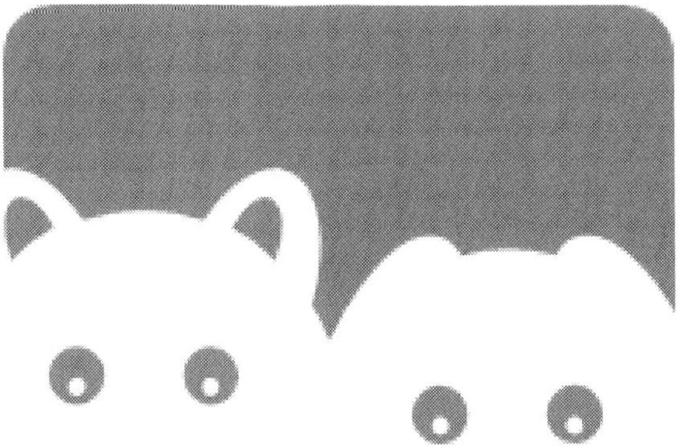

The Shih Tzu
SOLIDARITY

HARMONIOUS
ARROGANCE AND ATTENTIVNESS
AN ENGAGEMENT OR PARTNERSHIP
Two of Hearts

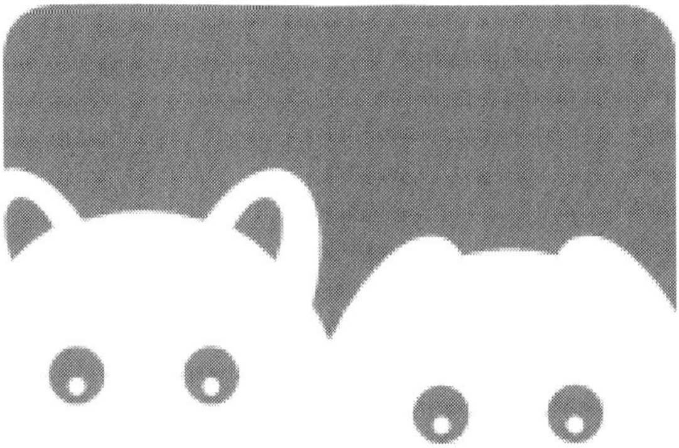

The Pet Psychic™

Have you ever wished you could talk to the animals? The Pet Psychic™ Canine Oracle Cards can facilitate the communication between you and your canines on earth as well as those who have crossed over. Communicate with your canine spirit guides as well as your canines, past and present with the help of The Pet Psychic™ **Canine Spirit Guide Oracle Cards**. Canines are often referred to as man's best friends, but they are really so much more than that. They offer us guidance, comfort and protection both here and in the afterlife. Canine Spirit Guides are powerful spirits that stay with us for lifetimes. As we connect with them we benefit from their loving wisdom and super-sensory abilities. Ron Ash's deck of 52 oracle cards will help facilitate your connection with canine spirit guides who are able to give advice in all areas of your life. Whether you are a novice or expert you'll love the ease and accuracy of these amazing diving tools.

Printed in Great Britain
by Amazon